IRELAND
ENGLAND
FRANCE
SPAIN
AFRICA
CANARY ISLES
AF371465

THREE SHIPS COME SAILING

A Child's Story of Our Country's Birthplace

JAMESTOWN IN VIRGINIA

By GILCHRIST WARING

Pictures by ELMO JONES

THE DIETZ PRESS, Richmond, Virginia

Printed in the United States of America

With deep appreciation to the Association
for the Preservation of Virginia Antiquities—
that group of patriotic women who have
labored so long and so faithfully to preserve
for us our country's birthplace.

To Our Young Readers:

COUNTRIES, like persons, have birthdays and birth-places. The thirteenth of May is our country's birthday, and Jamestown, on the north bank of the James River in Virginia, is her birthplace. This little story is about Jamestown—and we hope you will love it as much as we have loved preparing it.

THE AUTHOR AND THE ARTIST.

One cold December day, nearly three hundred and fifty years ago, three ships sailed out from the port of Blackwall, England. They were the Discovery, the Godspeed, and the Susan Constant, and aboard were about one hundred Englishmen and three or four English boys. These men and boys were bold adventurers who were sailing to the new country of Virginia in North America to start an English colony.

The people in England had heard many strange stories about the faraway country of Virginia. It was a land rich in gold and precious stones, the home of red-skinned

Indians, and a vast wilderness where savage beasts roamed through the forests.

Aboard the ships the Englishmen talked amongst themselves about the adventures that lay ahead. Some boasted of how they would gain fortunes and return home to live like princes. Others spoke of their hopes to Christianize the Indians. Then, there were those who talked only of their eagerness to start the new colony. Little did they dream that before them lay untold hardships, disappointments, and suffering. Still less did any of them dream that they were sailing to the new world to begin what would one day be a mighty nation—our United States of America!

In those days ships were small and frail, and the voyage was long and dangerous. Storms arose and tossed the vessels about on the mountainous waves. Some of the men, becoming seasick and frightened, wished to turn back. But others held fast to their courage and the three little ships sailed on.

In the following month of May, the adventurers entered a wide Virginia river which they named James in honor of their king. How good it felt to see the land again! They soon forgot the long, fearful voyage, and their hearts grew light as they sailed up the river searching for a landing place. About forty miles from the river's mouth they found a small peninsula where the water near the shore was deep enough to moor their ships. This spot they chose for their landing and named it Jamestown.

The Discovery, the Godspeed, and the Susan Constant were moored. Then the following morning, while trumpets blared, the exited colonists climbed ashore. It was springtime. Virginia was at her loveliest. The men were happy, indeed, and their minister, Mr. Robert Hunt, knelt and gave thanks to God for their safety.

Later, the settlers stretched and nailed to some trees a piece of old rotten tent under which Mr. Hunt held his services. They used logs and planks for seats and a bar of wood for the pulpit. This, it is said, was the first English church in the big Virginia wilderness.

At first the colonists camped in tents or under the trees. Within a few weeks, however, they had built some crude huts, a fort of boughs, a storehouse, and a chapel. Near the fort they had planted corn which was now growing tall and green under the Virginia sun. And this, in the summer of 1607, was the beginning of Jamestown— England's first permanent settlement in North America.

Each day curious Indians came to watch the building

of the fort and the village. The Indians, dressed in animal skins and decorated with shells, beads, and feathers, must have looked strange, indeed, to the Englishmen. But our adventurers must also have appeared strange to the Indians. The Englishmen had short hair and long unshaven beards. They wore knee breeches, Irish stockings, ruffs of plaited linen about their necks, and tight-fitting doublets.

At first the Indians were friendly. Soon, however, they began to suspect that the white men had come to drive them from their forests, and the thought of losing their homes filled them with hatred and anger. One day a band of painted warriors, seeing a group of unarmed colonists at work, attacked them with bows and arrows.

And before the surprised colonists had time to arm and defend themselves, the Indians had killed a boy and wounded several men. After this the adventurers protected their village with mounted cannon and strong palisades, or tall fence of pointed logs. They were careful, too, about going outside the fort without the protection of firearms.

During the summer Captain Christopher Newport, who was in charge of the little fleet, sailed for England with the Godspeed and the Susan Constant. He went to take news of the colony and to bring back provisions.

When Newport left all was well with the men at Jamestown. But another hardship, worse than Indian warfare, was coming to plague them. The land around Jamestown was marshy, low, and unhealthful. And when the weather grew warm the adventurers, unused to the climate, became ill with a fever. There were no doctors in the settlement. Had there been, the doctors in those days knew little about diseases and medicine. As the hot weeks dragged by, most of the men became too ill to work. They could no longer hunt and fish. Their food supply ran low. And before cold weather came to stop the fever, nearly fifty of our one hundred colonists had died.

The voices about the fort were no longer cheerful.

Many of the men had become homesick, discouraged, and lonely. Virginia was not the land of romance they had expected. Instead of gold and precious stones, they had found only the dreaded fever and the deadly Indian arrow.

Some of the adventurers, however, refused to lose hope. They still believed that, in spite of hardships, they could start an English colony. One of these was a young man called Captain John Smith. Smith was brave, wise, and fearless. During the summer he had worked hard to help those who were hungry and sick. And in December of that first difficult year, he set out through the wintry Virginia wilds to try to get food from the unfriendly Indians.

13

There is a story that on this trip some Indians captured Smith and took him to Werowocomoco on the York River. Werowocomoco was the winter home of the great Indian chief who was called the Powhatan. The Indians led Smith before the Powhatan who sat on a throne of boughs covered with the hides of raccoons. The old king looked fierce and sour, and surrounding him were shouting warriors and Indian women and children. Captain Smith, looking at the grim old king and hearing the blood-curdling shouts of the warriors, lost all hope for his life.

True enough, some of the braves dragged Smith close to the king and forced his head down on a stone. A warrior raised his club to strike. Then, we are told, the king's little daughter, Pocahontas, rushed through the crowd and begged without fear for the young man's life. At first this angered the sour old king, but at last he granted the princess' wish and spared the life of John Smith.

As soon as the Indians released Smith he returned to Jamestown where he found all in confusion. The leaders were bickering and quarreling. The food supply had run low. The crude huts offered poor shelter against the cold weather. And the settlers were more than ever discouraged.

One day, to the amazement of all, a strange procession of Indians, led by Pocahontas, entered the gate of the fort. On their shoulders, they carried baskets of corn and venison which they gave to Smith for the hungry men. After this, Pocahontas returned every four or five days with provisions. So, during that first bitter winter, the little Indian princess did much to help keep life in the settlers.

In January Captain Newport returned in the Susan Constant with a supply of food and about one hundred and twenty new colonists. At sight of the ships the men gave shouts of joy! They knew that with Newport's return, relief at last had arrived!

A few weeks later, however, another calamity came. No one knows quite how it happened, but Jamestown was burned. Food and clothing vanished in the flames. The men were forced to rebuild their homes. And as they worked, they must have thought again and again of their foolish dreams of riches.

In April Newport sailed again, carrying this time a shipload of yellow dirt. It was thought in both England and the colony that the yellow dirt contained gold, but how great was the disappointment of all when it was found to be only common clay!

In the fall Newport returned with about seventy new colonists. Much to the surprise of all, he brought also two women—Mrs. Forrest and her maid, Ann Burrass. These were the first women to join the Jamestown colony. And the first English marriage in Virginia was that of John Laydon and Ann Burrass.

During the second fall at Jamestown, Captain Smith was made president of the colony. While he was president he managed to keep order and provide enough food to keep the settlers from starving. This was not always easy, for some of the men were too lazy to work and others were jealous and quarrelsome. Smith made a rule that

17

those who would not work should not eat. And once he made a rule that a can of cold water be poured down the sleeve of anyone heard cursing.

The Indians had learned both to love and to fear Smith. They loved him for his courage and daring and feared him because he could outwit them. Smith had learned that the Indians would trade provisions for trinkets, beads, and copper, and had it not been for the food which he bought from them, the entire colony might easily have perished.

When Jamestown was a little more than two years old, Captain Smith returned to England. Some say he went home because he had been badly burned by an explosion of gunpowder. Others say that the constant bickerings and jealousies had at last wearied him. Whatever the cause, when Smith left, the colony lost one of her wisest leaders.

By this time about five hundred men, women, and children lived in Jamestown and the nearby settlements. Within the Jamestown stockade were a few frame dwellings, a frame church, and a storehouse. There was food enough to last for some time if it were wisely used, and everyone felt that success at last had come to the colony.

Smith, however, had been gone only a short time before

Jamestown was in hopeless confusion. New quarrels began. New jealousies broke out. And the leaders that followed Smith knew little about keeping peace and order.

When the Indians heard that Smith had left, they no longer feared the white men. Here and there they went, pillaging and killing. No one dared to venture beyond the palisades, and those who lived in the new settlements rushed to Jamestown for protection.

When winter came the hardships of the colonists grew worse. Due to poor management and the constant thieving of the Indians, the food supply ran out. Part of the fort was burned. The Indians, seeing a chance to be rid of the white men, refused to give help. Then what has long been known as The Starving Time set in at Jamestown. For food the poor hungry people had little more than a few fish, bark from the trees, roots, and acorns. Some died of sickness, and others of exposure and starvation. Sad to say, of the five hundred cheerful colonists who had bid Captain Smith good-bye in September, there remained in the following March only a wretched sixty!

Day after day, the starving settlers watched for a ship from England. At last, in the month of May, they sighted sails! A ship! Two ships were seen coming!

What piteous cries of rejoicing rose from the fort!

Strangely enough, the names of the ships were the Patience and the Deliverance. Aboard were Admiral Somers and Sir Thomas Gates who, in sailing from England to Virginia, had been shipwrecked in the Bermuda Islands. With their own hands they had built the ships in which to continue their journey. Now, since they had brought little in the way of food, they soon gave in to the pleadings of the settlers to take them home to England.

At the gate of the fort they buried the guns and cannon. Then to the doleful roll of drums they climbed

aboard the ships. Somers, fearing that the unhappy men might burn the remaining buildings, was the last to go aboard. A volley was fired. . . The sails were spread. . . The ships dropped slowly down the river. . .

And Jamestown, just three years old, was being deserted!

The faces of the weary colonists were at last turned homeward. For the first time in months they felt there was reason for hope and joy. Then, as they neared the mouth of the river, one of the strangest of all things happened—they met Lord Delaware coming with three shiploads of new colonists and provisions!

Delaware, sent from England as Virginia's first real governor, at once ordered Somers to return with the settlers to Jamestown. When Delaware landed and saw the crumbling, deserted fort, he knelt and gave thanks that he had come in time to save England's dying colony.

Delaware, a fearless leader, gave new hope to the colonists. Loving cleanliness and order, he commanded the men to repair the fort, clean the streets, and rebuild their houses. He had the church decorated with gay spring flowers. And twice each day the church bell rang to call the settlers to services.

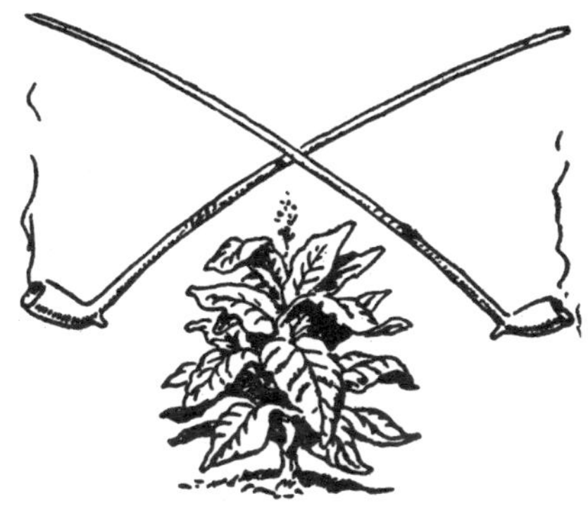

The new governor had brought food enough for all. In addition, he was clever enough to trade for supplies with the Indians.

The following spring Lord Delaware became ill and returned to England. During his few months in Virginia, however, he had restored order and life to the colony. He had built two new forts. And Jamestown, now thriving, was never again to be deserted.

After Captain John Smith left Virginia, Pocahontas no longer visited Jamestown. But later the English captured the princess and brought her to the fort as a prisoner. The colonists thought they could force the Powhatan to ransom his daughter by the return of some settlers and firearms the Indians had captured. The Powhatan released the settlers. He refused, however, to return the firearms and the princess remained a prisoner.

Living at Jamestown, Pocahontas learned to wear English clothes and to speak the English language. She gave up the Indian religion, became a Christian, and was re-named Rebekka. Then, she and John Rolfe, one of the colonists, fell in love and were married. The Powhatan, being pleased with the marriage, sent Indian relatives to witness the wedding which took place in the month of April in the little frame church at Jamestown.

For a time, the marriage of Pocahontas brought peace with the unfriendly Indians. So the unusual wedding brought much rejoicing, both in Virginia and England.

At first the colonists were disappointed that they had not found gold and precious stones in Virginia. From the Indians, however, they learned to grow tobacco. And within a few years they were raising and shipping it home to England.

Tobacco soon became so valuable it was used for money. And, sent to England, it could be exchanged for gold and precious stones or anything the settlers wanted.

Before long, tobacco was being planted everywhere. It was planted in fields along the rivers. It was planted in forest clearings. And, we are told, it was planted even in the streets of Jamestown! Now, the Indians no longer sold tobacco to the colonists—they came to the colonists to buy.

As news of the tobacco wealth spread, more and more Englishmen rushed to Virginia to settle. To gain wealth, they so neglected their other crops that the governor was at last forced to make a rule that a colonist must plant some corn each time he planted tobacco.

Until 1619, all laws for the Virginia colonists had been made for them in England. Now it was decided that they might be allowed to help make some of their own laws. What a glorious day this was! When the good news crossed the ocean, it must have given to each man and woman in the colony a feeling of pride and freedom.

The people chose, from different parts of Virginia, a few men who were to help the governor make the laws. These men, called Burgesses, met with the governor in the little church at Jamestown. Here it was, in the summer of 1619, that the first laws were made by Englishmen in North America.

There was a law that if one spoke ill of a neighbor he might be tied to a whipping post and given several lashes on the bare back. There was a law that no pleasure trip could be taken on Sunday—everyone must attend church. There was also a law against cursing and swearing.

During the year 1619, a Dutch ship anchored at Jamestown. On it were about twenty Negroes whom the Dutch sold to the settlers as slaves. Help was so badly needed in the tobacco fields that the colonists were glad enough to buy the Negroes. This was the beginning of Negro slavery in North America.

At this time there were still few women in the colony, and it was thought if the men could have wives they would be more contented. So, a ship carrying ninety women was sent from England to Jamestown.

ELMO
JONES

JAMESTOWN ABOUT 1620

What a day this was for the lonely Virginia bachelors!

Down to the wharf they came dressed in their best and eager to meet the ship bearing the maidens. Before any man could claim his bride, however, he must pay for her passage with one hundred and twenty pounds of tobacco. This each lucky man was happy enough to do and everyone in Jamestown became busy with weddings.

The plan was such a success that other women were sent over. And as the years passed, the voices of women and children could be heard throughout the colony.

As the planters settled farther and farther up the rivers, clearing new lands and building new homes, they pushed the Indians deeper and deeper into the forests. This further angered the natives, and Opechancanough, who had be-

28

come the Indian ruler in that part of Virginia, laid a secret
plot to wipe out the entire English colony. The plot of
this cunning ruler may have succeeded had it not been for
the wisdom and courage of an Indian boy, Chanco, who
had become a Christian and was living with an Englishman
across the river from Jamestown. Young Chanco revealed
the deadly plot in time for those who lived in and near
Jamestown to be warned and save themselves. In the dis-

tant settlements, however, the enraged Indians killed more than three hundred women, children, and men.

Although Indian warfare along the frontiers continued, the Virginia colony prospered. As time passed, the planters began to build six and seven-room houses, and each had a wharf of his own where ships could stop to unload provisions and take on tobacco.

Most of the early Virginians lived on plantations. No cities grew up and even Jamestown remained just a village. At Jamestown, however, the colonists had built a new brick church, a few brick dwellings, and a State House where the Burgesses met with the governor.

The early Virginians used candles for lights, and for heat and cooking had only the big, open fireplace. Everyone had knives, spoons, and pewter dishes, but only a few of the wealthiest had forks. For telling time, they used the hour-glass and sun-dial.

There were no public schools, so the children of the poor had little or no education. The wealthy planters had tutors for their children and some sent their sons, when they grew older, to attend schools in England.

The young people had little in the way of amusement. They loved to dance, however, and dances were often given on the big plantations. To please the merry-makers on these gay occasions, faithful servants would often fiddle till daybreak.

As the years passed, fashions changed. And as the colony prospered, the Virginians bought finer clothing. The men shaved their beards and wore powdered curls that hung to their shoulders. At church and fashionable gatherings they wore steepled hats, coats to the knees, fancy waistcoats, plush knee trousers, sleeves ending in ruffles, and shoes with silver buckles.

The women dressed even finer. On gay occasions they wore silk flowerd gowns, petticoats trimmed with silver

lace, brilliant scarfs, and mantles of crimson taffeta. They carried beautiful fans, and wore jewelry of silver, gold, and pearls. The children were dressed almost like their mothers and fathers.

The colonists sent to England for much of their clothing and many of their household articles. Up and down the rivers sailed the busy English ships, carrying to the planter's wharf the things he had ordered, and taking away the tobacco that usually was sent in payment.

Jamestown was burned four times during the ninety-one years it remained Virginia's capital. The fourth time was in 1698, when the State House and prison were burned. Then Middle Plantation, which was only a few miles from Jamestown, was selected as a new site for the capital. So the following year the capital was moved and, in honor of King William III, its name was changed from Middle Plantation to Williamsburg.

After Williamsburg became Virginia's capital, Jamestown, our country's birthplace, fell into ruins and for many years was almost forgotten. Streets became deserted. One by one the remaining houses tumbled down. And as time went by, the water of the James came up and ate part of the very land itself away.

There can still be seen at Jamestown the foundations of the old State House and a collection of colonial relics. The tower of the old brick church still stands looking quietly across the water. In recent years two statues have been placed near the old church tower, one of Captain Smith, the other of Pocahontas.

A seawall has been built to stop the eating away of the land by the water. On this seawall one may stand, look down the James, and in fancy see again three small ships— the Discovery, the Godspeed, and the Susan Constant.

They are small and frail, these ships, but they carry a precious cargo. They carry one hundred or more Englishmen and three or four adventuresome boys. These men and boys have crossed the ocean to fight untold hardships and suffering in the big Virginia wilderness as they begin our United States of America!

In 1893, the Association for the Preservation of Virginia Antiquities, a group of patriotic women and some men, became determined to save what was left of Jamestown. They set to work at once to preserve what was left of the ancient landmarks, and to have a seawall built to prevent further washing away of the land by the water. The Association for the Preservation of Virginia Antiquities and the National Park Service have taken care of Jamestown since 1940 under a coöperative agreement, and the historic Island is now open to the public at a nominal admission which is used for maintenance.

NORTH AMERICA
NEW ENGLAND
CHARTER BOUNDARY
VIRGINIA
JAMESTOWN
CHESAPEAKE BAY
CHARTER BOUNDARY
BERMUDA ISLES